To

_____

From

_____

Everyday Grace

FOR FRIENDS

60 DEVOTIONS

Ellie Claire® Gift & Paper Expressions
Franklin, TN 37067
EllieClaire.com
Ellie Claire is a registered trademark of Worthy Media, Inc.

Everyday Grace for Friends: 60 Devotions
© 2017 by Ellie Claire
Written by Jennifer Gerelds
Published by Ellie Claire, an imprint of Worthy Publishing Group, a division of
Worthy Media, Inc.

ISBN 978-1-63326-193-8

Stock or custom editions of Ellie Claire titles may be purchased in bulk for
educational, business, ministry, fundraising, or sales promotional use. For
information, please e-mail info@EllieClaire.com

Cover and interior art by Shutterstock.com

Cover and interior design by Jeff Jansen | AestheticSoup.com

Printed in China

1 2 3 4 5 6 7 8 9 HAHA 21 20 19 18 17

Contents

The secret of life

is that all we have and are

is a gift of grace to be shared.

LLOYD JOHN OGILVIE

Introduction

A friend loves you all the time.

PROVERBS 17:17 NCV

Even in Paradise—the Garden of Eden in its original, perfect condition—God knew Adam was missing something important, something integral to complete His creation. As beautiful and varied as the plants and animals were, none satisfied Adam's soul need for an earthly companion. Then God confirmed the truth He had Adam discover for himself: it's not good for humans to be alone. God wired each person for community—community with Himself, with our families, with our friends. Connection through friendship with God and each other is as essential to life as the very air we breathe.

In today's culture, though, true friendship can be hard to find. Endless social media outlets boast an instant connection. Who will really be there when times get tough? Who will brave the hard conversations when our own sin nature blinds us to the truth? Who will encourage and cheer us on to keep running the race God has put before us? Who will pray with us and for us?

Will we be *that* friend for others?

God tells us that true friends love at all times...not just the easy times, or the fun times, or the times when we are at our best. But as Jesus demonstrated while nailed to a cross, a true friend loves *at all times*. Thank God we have a friend like this in Jesus! May the Scripture promises in this book spark your courage to seek companions where you least suspect them and to cherish and sharpen those friendships that have already shaped you into who you are today. God, through you, will fill the world with everyday grace, changing lives one friendship at a time.

Day Brighteners

We must always thank God for you, brothers and sisters.
This is only right, because your faith is growing
more and more, and the love that every one
of you has for each other is increasing.

2 THESSALONIANS 1:3 NCV

Oh, she just texted me again, you realize as you glance down at
your phone. One of your friends is giving a daily update.
Yesterday it was a local coupon she didn't want you to miss.
Today it is a verse that caught her attention. Each of them
are simple little lines, words on a screen. But the connection tells you something more.

Your friend is thinking about you. She knows you
well enough to both shoot the breeze and bring a depth of
thought to your day. She is a fellow believer, one you know
has your back—if you ever need it—because she believes in
you. In short, she is a gift, one of God's colorful ways He
brightens your day and shows His own delight in you. Don't
miss the miracle when your phone lights up! God has given
you friends to lighten the load and let you feel His love in
the instant connection.

Father, thank You for giving me friends who help me see
Your beauty in the middle of my day.

Without true friends,
the world is but a wilderness.

FRANCIS BACON

Friendship is a gift from God
that's blessed in every part...
born through love and loyalty...
conceived within the heart.

ANONYMOUS

Life Source

So, no matter what I say, what I believe,
and what I do, I'm bankrupt without love.

1 CORINTHIANS 13:1 MSG

Just for a moment, imagine our world without love. Not even a *hint* of it. Would it not be a living hell? Without even fully realizing it, we require and rely on some sense of goodness in ourselves and others to find purpose and significance each day.

But where do we get that goodness? In the brokenness of this world, where do we find real and lasting love?

First John tells us that love has a source, and that source is God (1 John 4:8). He is literally the embodiment of all the good and right and light our lives crave. No wonder Jesus tells us to keep connected to Him, like a branch that draws nourishment from a vine! To pour forth life to others, to bear the kind of fruit that heals and helps our world, we must first be drawing it into our own veins and letting God's love flow through our own hearts. When we receive His grace through the power of His Word and Spirit in us, we no longer drain the system. Instead, we pour out hope like a fountain, filled by God's never-ending love for us.

Jesus, I need You to fill me with Your love and truth so that I can extend it to others.

Blessed are they who tenderly seek to comfort another and never run out of compassion and grace.

JANET L. SMITH

Friendship has no name but love.

HABIB SAHABIB

He is your friend who pushes you nearer to God.

ABRAHAM KUYPER

The Supplier

*This same God who takes care of me will supply
all your needs from his glorious riches,
which have been given to us in Christ Jesus.*

PHILIPPIANS 4:19 NLT

Are you amazed by the online stores these days? No matter what you need to purchase, some of the big name retailers seem to magically carry your product, with promises to deliver it straight to your door in just a couple of days. It's no wonder that mom-and-pop shops and other local chains are fighting hard to keep up with the variety and convenience online sites provide.

However, even online searches come up empty when what you need can't be stocked on shelves. Courage, wisdom, and integrity still can't be bought. Love, hope, and peace are priceless treasures in constant demand yet remain elusive to most.

But not for the Christian. God opens His storehouses wide to His children and invites each one of us to ask Him for exactly the kind of help we need as it arises in our lives. With endless resources and swifter than prime delivery, God gladly answers our prayers with supernatural accuracy, guiding and directing our lives as He fills us with everything we truly need to live in a way that honors Him.

Father, I praise You because You alone provide the hope, love, and strength I need today.

He is the Source. Of everything. Strength for your day. Wisdom for your task. Comfort for your soul. Grace for your battle. Provision for each need.

JACK HAYFORD

The grace of God has only one catch. Like any other gift, the gift of grace can be yours only if you'll reach out and take it.

FREDERICK BUECHNER

Growing Friends

The seeds of good deeds become a tree of life;
a wise person wins friends.

PROVERBS 11:30 NLT

Experience tells you that not every place is fertile ground for growing good friendships. Sometimes friendships spring up when your activities or location coincide with someone else's, and mere proximity fosters a level of friendship. But as kids grow older or people move and lives change, so do the relationships. You realize some connections bloom only for a short season. But God knows we need more, and through His Word, He tells us how important it is that we invest time and energy cultivating relationships that last—friendships grown from the firm and fertile foundation of Jesus Christ.

Are you spending time cultivating fair-weather friendships simply to fill the passing days, or are you more intentional about the kind of friendships you grow? Are you waiting for something substantial to just spring up out of the blue, or are you tending to the daily doses of time and attention required for real and lasting beauty? Ask the Lord of the harvest to show you how to improve your gardening skills, and to bless you with the bounty of strong friendships rooted in Him.

Lord, please give me strong friendships that last, and help me grow closer to You.

In friendship is a fragrant garden,
There are flowers of every hue.
Each with its own fair beauty
And its gift of joy for you.

ANONYMOUS

Character is so largely affected by associations
that we cannot afford to be indifferent as to who
and what our friends are. They write their names
in our albums, but they do more, they help make us
what we are. Be therefore careful in selecting them;
and when wisely selected, never sacrifice them.

M. HULBURD

Let those be thy choicest companions who have made
Christ their chief companion.

THOMAS BROOKS

Lighten Up

*Then, by the will of God, I will be able to come
to you with a joyful heart, and we will be
an encouragement to each other.*

ROMANS 15:32 NLT

Throughout the day, you've felt the tension mount. Pressures at home and stress at work have wormed their way from the pit of your stomach to the subtle frown on your face. But at last you make it home, and by some stretch of a miracle a meal is ready and the members of your family gather around the table to eat it together.

And then it happens. Conversation starts to flow, the pressure valve opened to release the day's steam. Moments in your day that initially seemed taxing now sound much funnier in the retelling. Suddenly, in sharing the day with loved ones, the worry lines on your face now frame the smile forming there. Laughter erupts, and the day is saved.

As you stop to thank God for daily food, thank Him, too, for the daily doses of joy He brings our way when we choose to recognize and receive them. God, Creator of the universe, is also Author of our laughter, and He loves to hear us relax and enjoy His goodness with others around us, right in the midst of our crazy world.

Lord, I confess I often see You as serious and forget that You created all things fun, too. Thank You for the gift of laughter with family and friends.

Yet he proved he is real by showing kindness,
by giving you rain from heaven and crops at the right
times, by giving you food and filling your hearts with joy.

ACTS 14:17 NCV

Grace creates liberated laughter. The grace of God...
is beautiful, and it radiates joy and awakens humor.

KARL BARTH

Give me a sense of humor, Lord,
Give me the grace to see a joke,
To get some happiness from life,
And pass it on to other folk.

JAMES METCALFE

Power House

He said to me, "My grace is enough for you.
When you are weak, my power is made perfect in you."
So I am very happy to brag about my weaknesses.
Then Christ's power can live in me.

2 CORINTHIANS 12:9 NCV

Almost every ardent student knows the struggle. Pastors, teachers, and leaders feel it, too. Maybe more than anyone, parents contend with daily reminders of one certain fact: life, and the hearts of people in it, lie outside our ability to control. Though we desperately want to play God as we try to dictate life's events, reality reveals our utter impotence. We are weak, vulnerable, and in need of an outside source of more dependable and formidable strength.

Fortunately, God's children have inherited such power. Though we still move about our day in our bodies as "jars of clay" (as Scripture puts it), we house an eternal power greater than the universe in which we live. As we let go of the prideful notion that our clay can accomplish anything of value on its own and instead cast all our hope and dependence on God, who works wonders through His Spirit in us, we find ourselves powerful. Indeed, enough to tear down every stronghold that sets itself up against a true knowledge of the only One who is great (2 Corinthians 10:5).

Lord, I gladly admit my desperate need for You. Fill me with Your Spirit that I may walk with power in all Your ways.

Grace is given not because we have done good works,
but in order that we may be able to do them.

ST. AUGUSTINE

This foolish plan of God is wiser
than the wisest of human plans,
and God's weakness is stronger
than the greatest of human strength.

1 CORINTHIANS 1:25 NLT

Crowned by Divine Right

What, then, shall we say in response to these things?
If God is for us, who can be against us?

ROMANS 8:31 NIV

Imagine you are a contestant in a beauty contest. You primp and prepare backstage with the rest of the contestants for the national competition everyone had been waiting for. But as they call your name and you walk out onto the stage, you cannot believe your eyes. There, sitting in the judges' seats, are your own loving parents—the very ones who told you to enter the competition in the first place. Your mind reels. Can this be fair? Doesn't everyone know that the judges are extremely biased—in my favor? You wonder. *How can I do anything but win?!*

While such conflicts of interest could never stand in an earthly competition, heaven operates by different rules. Your heavenly Father, who loved you from before time began, has chosen you to be His own child, clearing your record from all wrongs and crowning you with power from on high through faith in Jesus. The Judge of the universe has declared you victorious, without a single act to impress Him—save the simple belief that His grace is all yours for the taking through Jesus. If you lived today believing that God is already and completely for you, how would it impact the way you walk across life's stage?

God, I take great comfort knowing You are my greatest champion.

Grasp the fact that God is for you; let this certainty
make its impact on you in relation to what you
are up against at this very moment; and you will find
in thus knowing God as your sovereign protector,
irrevocably committed to you in the covenant of grace,
both freedom from fear and new strength for the fight.

J. I. PACKER

Friendship makes sacrifices, but asks nothing.

EMMANUEL VON GEIBEL

Focal Point

*I look up to the hills, but where does my help come from?
My help comes from the Lord, who made heaven and earth.*

PSALM 121:1-2 NCV

He had the right idea—at first. As all the terrified disciples gawked at what they first feared was a ghost walking to them on the water, Peter recognized Jesus and asked to join Him on the waves. Jesus beckoned and Peter defied all odds, walking on stormy water toward the Source of his new superpower. But as the waves danced higher, Peter's gaze diverted, sinking all his former glory.

Fortunately, Jesus never lost His focus or His grip. He saved Peter and rebuked them all for seeing their circumstances as greater than their sovereign Savior. Sometimes, like the disciples, even our friends can't help us navigate some of the tumultuous turns God calls us to take in life. But Jesus always can. And as a Good Shepherd, He always will. Don't let your eyes lose their focus on the only One who can save you in this moment, and who has already rescued you for all of time. Jesus is the constant companion who never fails to deliver the purpose, power, and perseverance we need to walk through life's storms with His grace.

Jesus, You have promised to never let go of me, so I will always keep my eyes on You!

When we focus on God, the scene changes.
He is in control of our lives; nothing lies outside
the realm of His redemptive grace. Even when
we make mistakes, fail in relationships,
or deliberately make bad choices, God can redeem us.

PENELOPE J. STOKES

Amongst true friends
there is no fear of losing anything.

JEREMY TAYLOR

By friendship you mean
the greatest love, the greatest
usefulness, the most open
communication, the noblest
sufferings, the severest truth,
the heartiest counsel,
and the greatest union of minds
of which brave men
and women are capable.

JEREMY TAYLOR

Open Up

They celebrate your abundant goodness
and joyfully sing of your righteousness.

PSALM 145:7 NIV

It's the crowning moment of every birthday party, and eager kids all gather around to watch it unfold. Presents, wrapped neatly with beautiful paper, stand ready to be ripped open and received with joyful wonder and thanks.

Of course, the celebration is a lot clearer when it comes with a bold invitation. But what about the gifts God tucks away into our day with much more subtlety? Do we notice the way the lights turned green at every intersection as we raced our way against all odds to be on time to work? Did we feel the warmth of our toddler's touch as he wrapped his small arms around ours? Did we hear the chatter of beautiful birds and feel the soothing breeze as overhead clouds scurried by? Did we perceive our friend's comfort as the tender touch of God?

With God, every day holds wonder, every encounter with our Creator and His creation an opportunity to open a new discovery into the heart of God. Will you savor the moments and remember the Giver of all good gifts is God Himself?

God, everything good in my life comes first from Your loving heart and hand. Thank You!

Thank you, God, for little things
That often come our way,
The things we take for granted
But don't mention when we pray.
The unexpected courtesy,
The thoughtful kindly deed,
A hand reached out to help us
In the time of sudden need.
Oh, make us more aware, dear God,
Of little daily graces
That come to us with sweet surprise
From never-dreamed-of places.

ANONYMOUS

To be grateful is to recognize the Love of God
in everything He has given us—and He has given us
everything. Every breath we draw is a gift of His love,
every moment of existence is a gift of grace.

THOMAS MERTON

Winter Winds

*We know that in everything God works
for the good of those who love him.*

ROMANS 8:28 ICB

In C. S. Lewis's *The Lion, the Witch, and the Wardrobe*, the characters first encounter Narnia when it is in a constant state of winter. Everything is frozen, including some of the creatures they discover as the adventure unfolds. But when Aslan arrives, warm winds of change begin to blow, and the budding of spring appears all the more vivid as it bursts forth from what once seemed so dead.

Lewis chose a season to show us an important truth about our lives in the real world. Because of sin and brokenness, we must expect to encounter difficult feelings of lifelessness or pain along our path. It may look like God has abandoned us or we will never escape our misery, shivering from the cold in the stark shadows of sorrow. But what lies below life's frozen surface is a phenomenal power. God is at work, forging pattern and purpose to every felt pain. He is working in His time a sensational beauty in us and the world around us that He will reveal when the time is right. So trust Him now, even though your faith feels cold. The warmth of His love never fails. The new life of joy that lies ahead boasts more brilliance than our best imagination.

God, thank You for working out everything in my life for my good. By faith I trust and will wait for You.

As it is written: "What no eye has seen, what no ear has heard, and what no human mind has conceived"— the things God has prepared for those who love him."

1 CORINTHIANS 2:9 NIV

Grace grows best in winter.

SAMUEL RUTHERFORD

For when we enter the fellowship of His sufferings, God strips us of our self-help mindset. We are forced to our knees and driven to lean on His grace. Then, and it seems only then, can God impart His Son's character to us. In so doing, we are made like Him.

JONI EARECKSON TADA

Trust and Obey

If you love me, obey my commandments.
JOHN 14:15 NLT

It's one thing to say you believe your doctor is the finest surgeon around. But it's quite another to willingly lie down on the operating table, entrusting your life to his hands. The difference lies between our words and the action that proves our words true.

Faith, has varying levels. We Christians are quick to avow our faith in Jesus as the risen Son of God, and we are right to do so. We enjoy hearing the promises of God and studying His Word along with other believers, another excellent investment of time. But God beckons us deeper still! God has called us to a living declaration of total dependence on Him. Faith in action no longer remains in study groups, but it expands to the world outside our home and church doors. It relies on God's promise to empower us with words and wisdom as we walk in His ways, being careful to listen for His Spirit as He directs our steps and leads us to the tangible works of God we were made to fulfill.

When we choose radical trust in God, life becomes a great adventure—the thrill of taking the miracle of reconciliation between God and His people to others all along your journey home. Today, accept God's invitation to deeper trust and extend it to others who want to know Him better, too.

Father, You are always faithful. Grow my faith by helping me follow You wherever You lead.

Faith is a living, daring confidence
in God's grace, so sure and certain that we
could stake our life on it a thousand times.

MARTIN LUTHER

[God] is looking for people who will come
in simple dependence upon His grace,
and rest in simple faith upon His greatness.
At this very moment, He's looking at you.

JACK HAYFORD

A Better Fortress

The name of the Lord is a strong fortress;
the godly run to him and are safe.

PROVERBS 18:10 NLT

You had trusted your friend with your heartfelt struggle, knowing you had nowhere else to turn. But today you got a call from someone else, someone who had "heard the news." Instantly you realized your security was breached. The friend you thought was faithful had failed you in a devastating way.

As wonderful as our friends can be, those closest to us can also cause the deepest pain when their words or actions wound us. In such times, it's so tempting to retreat from all forms of vulnerability, erecting walls between us and the world beyond to shut out the judgment, misunderstanding, and hurt. But Jesus invites us to a safer, better place of refuge—Himself. As our best Friend, He never fails us. He strengthens us with His power, comforts us with His love, and reminds us of who we are in Him.

And because Jesus always loves us and forgives us for our failures, we gain the courage to not only lower our defenses, but to defy the enemy's divisive tricks by forgiving anyone who offends us. God's grace toward us shows us what real love looks like. And by that same grace, we can keep loving others.

Jesus, if anyone knows what it feels like to be betrayed, it's You. Help me to be like You as I continue to forgive and love others who have hurt me.

Forgiveness is not acting as if things are just
the same as before the offense. We must face
the fact that things will never be the same.
By the grace of God they can be a thousand times better,
but they will never again be the same.

RICHARD J. FOSTER

Two persons will not be friends long
if they cannot forgive each other's little failings.

JEAN DE LA BRUYÈRE

Good Father

*Endure hardship as discipline; God is treating you
as his children. For what children are not disciplined
by their father?...They disciplined us for a little while
as they thought best; but God disciplines us for our good,
in order that we may share in his holiness.*

HEBREWS 12:7, 10 NIV

Anyone who has ever parented teens knows the potential pain they can inflict when obstructing their goals. No amount of logic or reason will soften their resolve, either. In the moment of discipline, teens can often see the situation only from their limited perspective, oblivious to the heart of love behind the rules the parent knows must be enforced for their own good.

The same short-sightedness and self-centeredness affects us as God's children, too. No matter how old we are, we buck like rebellious teenagers when God allows fiery trials to come our way. If we could call the shots, we'd certainly order peace and prosperity to rule the rest of our earthly lives.

But rest assured, each difficulty we encounter is ordained by our loving God to refine us, mold us into His image, and equip us to minister better to others in the same situation. Even though times are bad, God promises to work each moment for our good, as a good Father would. Will you trust Him in your trials today?

Father, You are always good and I trust You to complete the work You have begun in me.

Don't we all long for a father who, even though
our mistakes are written all over the wall, will love us
anyway? Don't we want a father who cares for us in spite
of our failures? We do have that type of a father. A father
who is at his best when we are at our worst. A father
whose grace is strongest when our devotion is weakest.

MAX LUCADO

We ought to give our friend pain if it will benefit him,
but not to the extent of breaking off our friendship;
but just as we make use of some biting medicine
that will save and preserve the life of the patient.
And so the friend, like a musician, in bringing about
an improvement to what is good and expedient,
sometimes slackens the chords, sometimes tightens them,
and is often pleasant, but always useful.

PLUTARCH

Upside Down

*God does not see the same way people see. People look
at the outside of a person, but the Lord looks at the heart.*

1 SAMUEL 16:7 NCV

If you're the competitive sort, you know the rules of the
game. Our culture constantly reminds us what it takes to
be on top, to make it to the enviable place of power and
prestige. And many fall prey to the lure, investing their
energy and money to be the one recognized for the greatest
achievements.

But God's vision for His people is quite different than
the rat race of an American dream. In fact, through Jesus we
discover our natural inclinations for power and position are
upside down. As Creator of the universe, Jesus didn't strive
to prove His worth or grapple with the Father for rights.
Instead, He obeyed, leaving the throne room of heaven to
enter into the problems and pains of ordinary people. If that
weren't enough, He humbled Himself by serving often hos-
tile, ungrateful people, giving His very life so that we could
all find freedom and forgiveness. From that position of total
humility, God the Father has exalted Him to the highest place.

Today when you feel the tug to assert your worth or put
your wants before others, follow God's lead instead. As you
humble yourself under God's hand, He will lift you up in
His time.

Lord, let there be more of You and less of me as I walk with
You and serve others today.

Be humble and give more honor
to others than to yourselves.
Do not be interested only in your own life,
but be interested in the lives of others.

PHILIPPIANS 2:5 NCV

Above all the grace and the gifts that Christ gives
to His beloved is that of overcoming self.

ST. FRANCIS OF ASSISI

Forever Fellowship

Father, I pray that they can be one. As you are in me
and I am in you, I pray that they can also be one in us.
Then the world will believe that you sent me.

Want to know what's so great about best friends? You can forget all the pretense and leave behind any pressure to perform. You understand one another and know what to expect. Whether talking or in silence, your soul is at rest, confident in the unbreakable bond you both share.

Have you ever considered why God gives us such good friends? After all, He's the one who placed the drive for deep fellowship inside us.

Everything about God shouts community. Father, Son, and Spirit—three persons in one God—have communed with one another in perfect unity for all of eternity. Made in God's image, we are invited by the Father through Jesus to join in that fellowship, His Spirit sealing the connection. When we recognize our permanent position in God's everlasting love, we enter into true rest and relaxation as we revel in His presence. Together with all of God's children, we discover the joy Jesus gives us through the fellowship and communion of God and His people.

Today, take time to enjoy God's presence, resting comfortably at peace in His love.

Thank You, Jesus, for inviting me to permanently belong in the family of God!

The goal of grace is to create a love relationship
between God and us who believe,
the kind of relationship for which we were first made.
And the bond of fellowship by which God
binds himself to us is His covenant.

J. I. PACKER

Human love and the delights of friendship,
out of which are built the memories
that endure, are also to be treasured up
as hints of what shall be hereafter.

BEDE JARRET

Passing Patience

Love is patient and kind.

1 CORINTHIANS 13:4 NLT

You don't even have to see the person's face to know how they feel. You can tell it by the way they have positioned their car right up on your bumper—even though you're going the speed limit. As they screech to the other lane and blast past you, you can't help but feel "put in your place." It's the subtle shaming that always comes with others' impatience.

How incredible is it, then, that our Creator abounds in patience toward His people? Though we are such slow learners, God patiently works to teach us His ways and conform us to the image of Christ. Unlike people, He is not in a hurry to get past us to His agenda. His agenda *is* us. He maximizes every moment for our good, and He's willing to wait until we can grasp how great His love for us really is.

The next time you feel the pressure of someone else's impatience, or when you're tempted to lose your temper with someone else, remember God's great patience with you. Thank Him and show your gratitude by extending His grace to the world around you.

God, You are never in a hurry because You work all things out in Your time. Please fill me with Your patience so I can love others better.

The essence of true friendship is to make
allowances for another's little lapses.

DAVID STOREY

If we refuse to treat people as our enemies,
we have the best possible chance
of winning them to be our friends.

CATHERINE GORE

There is nothing
on this earth more to be prized
than true friendship.

THOMAS AQUINAS

Three Steps Back

*He who began a good work in you will carry it on to
completion until the day of Christ Jesus.*

PHILIPPIANS 1:6 NIV

You thought you had been making progress. Just last week
you noticed that you didn't run your mouth (like usual)
when your neighbor complained about the length of your
grass. But today—today you blew it in the same way you
have a thousand times before and prayed you'd never do
again. Seeing the sin, such seeming lack of success, erodes
your confidence and makes you question the authenticity
of your faith. *What kind of Christian loses it like that?* you wonder.

The answer? All of us. Sinners saved by grace still battle
daily, moment by moment, to put off the old and put on the
new ways of Jesus. But do not be discouraged at the times
you lose the skirmish. Instead, recognize it for what it is: a
reminder of how much we need Jesus, not only for our eternal salvation but also for help in each and every moment.
Fortunately, not only is God patient and forgiving, He is all
powerful. And He has promised to perfect the work He has
begun in you. So even when it appears that no progress in
your life is being made, remember God's promise. He has
never failed to forgive the repentant, and He always finishes
what He starts!

Thank You, Jesus, that I can trust You to transform my
broken life into something beautiful for You.

I *am not what I ought to be,*
I am not what I wish to be,
I am not what I hope to be;
but, by the grace of God,
I am not what I was.

JOHN NEWTON

F*riendship is love with understanding.*

ANCIENT PROVERB

Off the Hook

So now there is no condemnation
for those who belong to Christ Jesus.

ROMANS 8:1 NLT

It wasn't until you passed that little side road where the patrol car hid that you noticed the number on your speedometer. Unfortunately, the policeman noticed, too, and flashed you down with his twirling blue lights and unmistakable siren. Out of any reasonable excuses, you roll down your window and await your fate. But to your great surprise, the officer lets you off the hook. Turns out he was friends with your parents! Your connection with them brought you unexpected grace.

And so it is for those who belong to Jesus. God "lets us off the hook" of guilt and condemnation for our own sins—not because He could ignore them, but because He paid the "ticket" at the cost of His Son's life so we could go free. Instinctively we know we don't deserve such divine affection. And sometimes we're tempted to try to earn the love that's already freely given, unwilling to receive such remarkable grace. But faith in God's goodness, not ours, honors the Father and shows the gratitude toward Him He desires from us. Today, thank God for freeing you from all your past, present, and future sins because of your connection with Jesus, and pray for His grace to help you follow Him.

Father, thank You for sending Jesus to pay a price I couldn't pay for my own sin. I receive Your grace with deepest thanks.

The beauty of grace, our only permanent
deliverance from guilt, is that it meets us
where we are and gives us what we don't deserve.

CHARLES R. SWINDOLL

God made him who had no sin to be sin for us,
so that in him we might become
the righteousness of God.

2 CORINTHIANS 5:21 NIV

On Track

*God is our refuge and strength, an ever-present help
in trouble. Therefore we will not fear, though the earth
give way and the mountains fall into the heart of the sea.*

PSALM 46:1-2 NIV

Do you know what makes roller coasters so fun? Even if they hold death-defying drops, you know those wheels are tethered by steel to the tracks on which they run. People pay good money for that adrenaline rush.

But no one forks out cash to feel the stressors of change in life. Whether we're starting something new or battling old baggage, our minds often fill with fears of future unknowns. After all, there's no guarantee your plan will stay glued to the tracks in real life.

But there is One who knows the future and He promises it will be good. Though at times it may feel like life has taken a wrong turn, an unexpected twist that derails where you thought you'd go, you can still soar through life worry-free in spite of your circumstances because of one important truth: your tracks are tethered to God through Christ. Though you may be shaken, He will never let you fall. Rely on God alone to guide and protect you, and you will experience lasting joy on the ride of your life.

Lord, I trust You with today and humbly give You all my worries. Have Your way with me today.

God's glorious grace says: *"Throw guilt and anxiety overboard, draw the anchor, trim the sails, man the rudder, a strong gale [of My Spirit] is coming!"*

CHARLES R. SWINDOLL

So do not fear, for I am with you; do not be dismayed, for I am your God. I will strengthen you and help you; I will uphold you with my righteous right hand.

ISAIAH 41:10 NIV

Loving Light

Your word is a lamp that gives light wherever I walk.

PSALM 119:105 CEV

On ordinary days, candles and flashlights don't mean that much to us when it comes to lighting up our lives. We have electricity and plenty of lamps and recessed lighting for that. But what about when the power goes out, even into the evening hours? Our appreciation for light takes on a whole new meaning!

The same is true with God's grace. Though we live by it every day, we often don't take note of it until we find ourselves in a desperately dark place and realize we require it. Wrong choices and real-life living in a broken world land us in some pretty dark, often terrifying valleys at times. But as believers, we are not undone. We have only to reach for the truth of God's presence and the brilliant hope of His promises to light the path in front of us. We can actually thank God in our frightening situations, because they forge a deeper faith within us. Without suffering, it seems, we'd never really recognize the beauty and necessity of God's grace.

Jesus, You are the light of my life. Thank You for leading me through the darkness.

God's grace is the oil that fills the lamp of love.

HENRY WARD BEECHER

*When I need a dose of wonder I wait for a clear night
and go look for the stars.... In the country the great
river of the Milky Way streams across the sky,
and I know that our planet is a small part of
that river of stars. Often the wonder of the stars
is enough to return me to God's loving grace.*

MADELEINE L'ENGLE

Accounting for Grace

I have hope when I think of this:
The LORD's love never ends; his mercies never stop.
They are new every morning; LORD, your loyalty is great.

LAMENTATION 3:21-23 NCV

Imagine sitting down at your desk to pay your bills. Checking your bank account online, you see you have just enough funds to cover the day's demands. And so you work your way through the stack, sighing intermittently with each transaction. But what if, when you woke up the next day, your balance was back up to where you started before? And the next day the same phenomenon happened again? And the next? Pretty soon you'd realize you no longer needed to worry about your funds. You are free to spend and free to give because somehow, miraculously, your financial reservoir is always refilled.

A similar freedom unfolds for all those who understand God's mercies. Unlike people, God doesn't hold grudges or keep record of wrongs. As His children, we enjoy the benefit of His presence and pleasure every single day. No matter how bad we blew it the day before, His mercies and love for us today are as full as ever. We simply can't deplete God's reservoirs of grace.

So how does this truth change us? We don't have to be cheap with others. We can lavish forgiveness and unconditional love, knowing that God—our source of giving—will never give out.

God, I look forward to each new day because You fill me once again with Your love and grace.

G*race...like the Lord, the giver,*
never fails from age to age.

JOHN NEWTON

I*f there has come to us the miracle of friendship,*
if there is a soul to which our soul has been drawn,
it is surely worthwhile being loyal and true.

HUGH BLACK

In Touch

When an actor wants to play a part well, he doesn't just read the script. He researches his character and the surrounding situations. He practices the gestures and mimics the tone. But the most dedicated take even more drastic measures, altering their weight or hair or even living conditions just to have a better understanding and feel for the person they're representing on camera.

God the Father had a role for Jesus to play in saving the world. But Jesus didn't do it from His comfortable throne in heaven. Beyond any exchange our world has ever seen, Jesus stripped Himself of sovereign glory to enter our world as a helpless baby, born to experience life as a human. And so He lived life like us, except with perfection where we would have failed. Now we have a Savior who not only rescues us, He relates to us! He understands what it is to feel tired, torn, beloved, and betrayed.

What temptation or struggle do you face today? Turn to Jesus, the One who left His comfort to feel your pain, and gives you power to overcome it.

Jesus, thank You for knowing exactly how to help me in my weakness and saving me in every way.

When God's Son took on flesh,
He truly and bodily took on, out of pure grace,
our being, our nature, ourselves. This was the eternal
counsel of the triune God. Now we are in Him.
We belong to Him because we are in Him.

DIETRICH BONHOEFFER

From the simple seeds of understanding,
we reap the lovely harvest of true friendship.

ANONYMOUS

Losing Baggage

Give all your worries and cares to God,
for he cares about you.

1 PETER 5:7 NLT

Airlines have increasing restrictions these days, particularly with luggage allowances. It's up to you to plan and pack wisely so that you can enjoy your trip with basic necessities from home without bringing everything you own with you. In the end, we often discover that our flights and stays are easier when we pack lighter.

The same is true with life. Daily we are bombarded with heavy issues, from chaos and turmoil in the global scene to relational and financial strife in our work and home. We face problems with kids, coworkers, neighbors, and church members. We battle insecurities and uncertain futures. Each concern carries its own considerable weight in our minds. Together, the baggage can bog us down so low in fear that we can't function.

But Jesus urges us to travel through life lightly. He invites us to cast not just some but all of our cares on God because He cares for us! When we begin to trust that God is far more capable than us and faithful than us to handle our issues correctly, we are freed to enjoy life's journey and help others with their burdens along the way.

Jesus, You don't add to my stress. You're the only one who relieves my heavy heart. Thank You for caring for me!

*The burden of life is from ourselves,
its lightness from the grace of Christ
and the love of God.*

WILLIAM B. ULLATHORNE

Grace is love that cares and stoops and rescues.

JOHN R. W. STOTT

Filling Up

The Lamb at the center of the throne will be their shepherd;
"he will lead them to springs of living water."
"And God will wipe away every tear from their eyes."

REVELATION 7:17 NIV

You've been working outside in your yard all morning when you suddenly start to feel weak, even a bit dizzy in the intensifying heat. Despite your goals to finish your project, you realize you won't make it that far if you don't take a break and replenish the fluids you've lost. But with hydration your body revives and you're ready for work again.

God designed His physical world in a way to help us see spiritual truths. Just as our bodies require water for life, our souls thirst for Living Water, heavenly refreshment found only through a relationship with Jesus. We may have all kinds of plans and goals for our day, but unless we drink of Jesus first and fill our hearts and minds with His Spirit and truth, we will not have the power we need. As believers, we must take the time to ingest God's goodness.

Do you set aside time each day to drink deeply from God's well of grace? Do you see it as a to-do to check off or a time of true fellowship? Ask God to anoint your time with His Spirit and turn your heart fully to Him each day so that you will feel refreshed for all that lies ahead.

Jesus, Your presence refreshes me like nothing else in this world. I praise You for being the Living Water!

From God, great and small, rich and poor,
draw living water from a living spring,
and those who serve Him freely and gladly
will receive grace answering to grace.

THOMAS À KEMPIS

Whoever believes in me, as Scripture has said,
rivers of living water will flow from within them.

JOHN 7:38 NIV

You, my people, have sinned in two ways—
you have rejected me, the source of life-giving water,
and you've tried to collect water in cracked
and leaking pits dug in the ground.

JEREMIAH 2:13 CEV

Friendship is born at that moment when one person says to another: What! You too? I thought I was the only one.

C. S. LEWIS

Hide and Seek

Seek first God's kingdom and what God wants.
Then all your other needs will be met as well.

MATTHEW 6:33 NCV

You've misplaced your keys—again. Dumbfounded, you leisurely check all the places you usually leave them, but they're not there. Then your phone lights up, reminding you of the doctor's appointment you have in thirty minutes, and it takes twenty-five minutes to get there. Suddenly your searching takes on a whole new level of urgency. In fact, everything else gets put on hold until you find the one thing you need most right now, because frankly, nothing else matters if you can't find your keys.

God wants us to pursue Him like that...not just casual glances for Him at church or maybe a weekly Bible study, but daily, intensely, and intentionally looking for His heart through time alone with Him in His Word and prayer. Like a reminder on our phone, the Bible urges us to seek God while He may be found, implying that we don't have all the time in the world. Search for Him like your life depends on it, because it actually does. Best of all, we can pursue Him with confidence that our efforts are never in vain. God promises to richly reward all those who seek Him by revealing who He really is.

Lord, nothing in life is more important than You. I commit to seeking You first.

God will...lead forward those who by His grace
see Him in His beauty and seek Him in His love.

A. W. TOZER

Seek the Lord while he may be found;
call on him while he is near.

ISAIAH 55:6 NIV

But if from there you seek the Lord your God,
you will find him if you seek him
with all your heart and with all your soul.

DEUTERONOMY 4:29 NIV

Living Grace

From his fullness we have all received, grace upon grace.

JOHN 1:16 ESV

How do you know you depend on something? When it's not there, you simply can't function without it. For example, imagine losing your phone this week without the ability to replace it. Would you be able to contact your friends? Coworkers? Find information? Find your destination? Losing your phone indefinitely would have a profound impact on your life.

So how can you tell if you depend on God? By measuring the impact on your life if He's not there. As connected as we can be with technology, God wants to be our first go-to for help and life. His gift of salvation doesn't wait to be opened at the gates of heaven. God intends to be our saving grace in the here and now. We not only need rescue from the eternal consequences of sin, we need power in the moment to overcome it daily and to make right choices that lead us and others closer to God. Thank God, He gives us the resource we need to stay in constant contact with Him: His Spirit through the power of prayer.

How is your prayer life? Does it reveal dependency on God or distraction with earthly resources? Ask God to help you grow more reliant on His power to rescue you today.

Father, in my head I know I need You. But help my heart to rely on You in reality.

Prayer is the deliberate and persevering action
of the soul. It is true and enduring,
and full of grace. Prayer fastens the soul
to God and makes it one with God's will,
through the deep inward working of the Holy Spirit.

JULIAN OF NORWICH

They who seek the throne of grace
Find that throne in every place;
If we live a life of prayer,
God is present everywhere.

OLIVER HOLDEN

The Place of Grace

*I always thank my God for you
because of the grace God has given you in Christ Jesus.*

1 CORINTHIANS 1:4 NCV

Your child just called you from school. She left her backpack at home and with it some important papers she really needs today. You already know the sacrifice in your agenda a trip home and to the school will cost you. Yet you extend your child grace and go anyway. Why? Because love—and the benefit it brings your child—matters more.

And so it is with God and His children. Solving our sin problem was no simple fix. Jesus, God's only Son, would have to suffer and die in our place, His sacrifice greater than any our minds could conceive. The Bible says Jesus did it for the joy that lay ahead of that terrible cross. To God, incredible pain and shame was worth paying for the reward of restored relationship with His people. The purpose for God's great grace in our lives is not only to clear our guilt, but to clear the path for eternal fellowship with our Father.

Because of our permanent position in God's love through Jesus, we can call on Him anytime, anywhere, and know that we have His help and His heart, every time we ask.

Father, thank You for pursuing me with all of Your heart. In response, I gladly give You mine.

Grace means God moving heaven and earth to save
sinners who could not lift a finger to save themselves.
Grace means God sending His only Son to the cross
to descend into hell so that we guilty ones might
be reconciled to God and received into heaven.

J. I. PACKER

Jesus suffered death on the cross. But he accepted
the shame of the cross as if it were nothing.
He did this because of the joy that God put before him.

HEBREWS 12:2 ICB

The Power of Prayer

When a believing person prays, great things happen.

JAMES 5:16 NCV

The disciples were in trouble. While Jesus had been away on a mountain revealing His deity to Peter, James, and John, the rest were wrestling with argumentative teachers and a demon-possessed boy. Despite their best efforts, they couldn't get the evil spirit to leave the child alone. But when Jesus arrived on the scene, He spotted the problem right away and called it out. The father's unbelief had hindered the miracle, but the disciples had failed to pray. Relying on their own strength, they were powerless to help.

Even today, faith (belief) works best with prayer. Trusting God sets our hearts toward Him for help. But in the asking, we tap into God's eternal power. He hears our prayers and answers in ways that are far beyond our own ability to accomplish.

If you have felt ineffective lately in your Christian walk, watch out for prayerlessness in your life. Remember to connect with your Father through prayer, asking Him for direction and power for each step of life. Then watch in wonder as God reveals His glory in the most unexpected ways.

Lord, please teach me how to pray at all times and for every situation. I need You every moment!

P*eople we can pray with make the best friends.*

JANETTE OKE

F*or the eyes of the Lord are on the righteous*
and his ears are attentive to their prayer.

1 PETER 3:12 NIV

Waiting on Purpose

*In the morning, LORD, you hear my voice; in the morning
I lay my requests before you and wait expectantly.*

PSALM 5:3 NIV

There are some (crazy) shoppers who take waiting in line to a whole new level. Days before Black Friday sales, they set up tents in store parking lots, all to secure their space in line first. Strangely, they've turned it into a fun event, enjoying camaraderie and conversation in the wait.

While they could probably get whatever deal they really wanted online anyway, there is a lesson they teach us that's more valuable than any doorbuster deal. And it's this: that sometimes we have to wait for what we want, and pleasure can be found in the process as well as the end objective. We would do well to approach prayer requests with the heart of a Black Friday shopper: Believe God's promises enough to camp out in the anticipation of their revelation. Don't give up waiting. And dare to be the first person in line to take God up on His offers.

What seemingly impossible prayer request do you have that tempts you to give up hope? Ask God today for His grace to not only wait while believing, but to enjoy the pleasure of His presence in the process.

Lord, even though I want You to answer me now, teach me to know You better as I wait for You to work.

*Give me, O God of my prayer,
the grace to continue waiting for You in my prayer.*

KARL RAHNER

*Oh, God, give me grace for this day.
Not for a lifetime, nor for next week, nor
for tomorrow, just for this day.
Direct my thoughts and bless them,
Direct my work and bless it...
So that for this one day, just this one day,
I have the gift of grace that comes from your presence.*

MARJORIE HOLMES

Sharing Secrets

All people will know that you are my followers
if you love each other.

JOHN 13:35 NCV

Shortly after Jesus ascended back to heaven and all His followers gathered together in Jerusalem per His instructions, God showed up in the most unexpected and powerful way. The people who had walked and served alongside Jesus were suddenly filled with His presence on the inside! The Holy Spirit arrived with such power it sounded like a mighty rushing wind and looked like flames of fire above each believer's head.

But the after-effects got everyone's attention. Those anointed believers began sharing the gospel with everyone around them—in languages they hadn't even learned. Most impressive of all was the way they now lived. No one cared about claiming power or possessions for themselves. Instead, they enjoyed time together in perfect unity, giving whatever they had to meet each other's needs, working together to further God's kingdom.

How can people today hear and believe the gospel? If we give of ourselves in the same sacrificial way. Only when we love others generously like Jesus will the world see the difference of Christ in us. Today, ask Jesus for more of His Spirit to help you live and love like Him.

Father, please fill me with Your Spirit so that I can love and serve others the way You want me to.

More about Jesus would I know,
More of His grace to others show;
More of His saving fullness see,
More of His love who died for me.

More about Jesus let me learn,
More of His holy will discern;
Spirit of God, my teacher be,
Showing the things of Christ to me.

ELIZA E. HEWITT

The Lord Jesus himself said:
"It is more blessed to give than to receive."

ACTS 20:35 NIV

Forgettable Gifts

One thing I do: forgetting what lies behind and reaching forward to what lies ahead, I press on toward the goal for the prize of the upward call of God in Christ Jesus.

PHILIPPIANS 3:13-14 NASB

We forget things all the time. We set down our phones, keys, or wallets only to wonder five minutes later where on earth we put them. We forget about doctor's appointments and parent-teacher meetings. We forget to take out the trash or pay bills on time.

But one thing we always seem to remember is our past mistakes. Regret can haunt us for the rest of our lives if we don't follow in the footsteps of the apostle Paul. He tells believers to just forget it! All those past failures and sins, those seemingly wasted years apart from God, need to be first confessed and then forgotten. Dwelling on the past doesn't help your progress. But shifting your focus to Jesus and the call of hope and righteousness in front of you does. Somehow, miraculously, God is powerful enough to redeem our past problems and work them for our future good.

Whenever you feel like beating yourself up for something you've done, tell God how grateful you are for His forgiveness instead. Then set your face like flint to follow Jesus, whose faithful love never fails. Your bright future with Him lies ahead!

Father, thank You for cleansing me from all my guilt and shame. I look forward to walking with You today!

You can never change the past. But by the grace of God, you can win the future. So remember those things which will help you forward, but forget those things which will only hold you back.

RICHARD C. WOODSOME

He does not treat us as our sins deserve or repay us according to our iniquities. For as high as the heavens are above the earth, so great is his love for those who fear him; as far as the east is from the west, so far has he removed our transgressions from us.

PSALM 103:10-12 NIV

Friends forget your defects, and if they are very fond of you, they don't see any.

ANONYMOUS

Personalized Paths

Since we have gifts that differ according to the grace given to us, each of us is to exercise them accordingly.

ROMANS 12:6 NASB

Flipping your favorite author's latest book release over, you read through her bio on the back cover. *How can a mother of six run her ministry, speak all over the world, write books, and get the laundry done while looking like a million dollars in the process?* you marvel. Suddenly you don't see her books as inspirational anymore. Now they are little missiles of guilt that make you wonder why your own life pales in importance by comparison.

And that, dear friend, is why God warns us not to compare our lives with others. The beauty of walking with Jesus is how He personalizes each person's path to fit with His unique calling on our lives. The race God says we are to run is not in competition with one another but in completion of each other. We must work together, each contributing whatever gift God has given us for the body of Christ to function as one unit loving the world well.

If you don't know what your gifts are, ask your family or friends. Take a spiritual assessment test. And ask your heavenly Father to show you. Then find freedom in relinquishing all other noble tasks and discover the pleasure of fulfilling your own life's purpose.

Lord, help me keep my eyes on You as I work through the work You've given me. To bring life and hope to a world that's desperate for it.

Friendship is something that raised us almost above humanity. This love, free from instinct, free from all duties but those which love has freely assumed, almost wholly free from jealousy, and free without qualification from the need to be needed, is eminently spiritual. It is the sort of love one can imagine between angels.

ANONYMOUS

But godliness with contentment is great gain, for we brought nothing into the world, and we cannot take anything out of the world.

1 TIMOTHY 6:6-7 ESV

I*f, instead of a gem*

or even a flower, we could cast

the gift of a lovely thought

into the heart of a friend,

that would be giving

as the angels give.

GEORGE MACDONALD

Saying Grace

What you say can mean life or death.
Those who speak with care will be rewarded.

PROVERBS 18:21 NCV

There's a reason we seek out our best friend when we are feeling down. We believe they'll know just what to say—and what not to say—to cheer us up and help us refocus. We rely on their encouragement to remind us who we really are according to God and not our record.

And such is the power of a timely word! It's truly amazing how much power God has packed into such a small, often unruly muscle in our mouths! What we choose to say to others has the power to inspire, affirm, encourage, and even exhort in love. But if we're not careful, our words can wield catastrophic damage. In a moment of anger toward others, we can annihilate their confidence, undermine their identity, and flatline any potential for future fellowship. Like squeezed-out toothpaste, our words can't be stuffed back in once they're out in the open. God warns us to watch our words carefully, for they carry the power of life and death inside them.

Do you need help controlling your tongue? God, Maker of your mouth, has the power to fill yours with His words of life. Ask Him today to help you spend your life building others up into Him.

Father, fill my heart with Your grace and my mouth with Your words of love.

Words can sometimes,
in moments of grace,
attain the quality of deeds.

ELIE WIESEL

There is nourishment from being encouraged
and held up by others when we are weak.
We are nourished from feedback from friends whom
we trust and who will be honest with us.

HUGH BLACK

Birthday Beauty

This means that anyone who belongs to Christ has become a new person. The old life is gone; a new life has begun!
2 CORINTHIANS 5:17 NLT

Months of planning and preparation, worry and wonder melt into a single moment of indescribable joy when your arms first cradle your newborn child. What a miracle of life! What a display of glorious design by the God whose image we bear. And what a beautiful picture of what heaven feels when, by God's grace, we are born again.

Becoming a Christian is not just a turning over of a new leaf or an attempt to get our act together. It's a moment of new birth. When we surrender our lives to the lordship of Jesus, the Bible says that the old is now gone. The new has come! We are raised to an entirely new life in Jesus, nourished now by His Spirit who lives inside us. Though our physical bodies look the same, heaven celebrates the very real spiritual birth that happens in our hearts.

Are you caught in a works-based religion, or have you surrendered your life to the lordship of Jesus? If not, commit your life to Jesus and receive His forgiveness. Then celebrate your birthday as a new creation in Christ!

Jesus, thank You for scrapping the old me and making me totally new in You!

True friendship gives new life and animation
to the object it supports.

M. HULBURD

I am about to do something new. See,
I have already begun! Do you not see it?
I will make a pathway through the wilderness.
I will create rivers in the dry wasteland.

ISAIAH 43:19 NLT

A newborn opens a door from God
and lets grace pour in.

ANONYMOUS

Speed Trap

Be still, and know that I am God! I will be honored
by every nation. I will be honored throughout the world.

PSALM 46:10 NLT

You are headed for the beach and you just can't get there fast enough. But throughout the backroads leading to Paradise is a number of small towns. If you clock 70 mph in those parts, you'll earn yourself a hefty ticket. To sail through unscathed, you often have to slow way down to a seeming crawl.

Slowing down doesn't happen naturally in our culture anymore. We all seem wired to fly at the speed of light, trying to somehow cram everything we can into too short of a day. Worse than getting a ticket, we miss God and important relationships when we insist on driving through life full throttle.

Like a stop sign would, God tells us in His Word to be still. In the stillness, we are to remember that He is God. He owns this world and everything in it, including our time. Paradise is not some goal to be achieved, it is the pleasure of His presence meant to be felt in this very moment, along with the people He has put in your path today.

Father, forgive me when I get ahead of You. Help me to be still and wait on You.

Prescription for a happier and healthier life:
Resolve to slow your pace; learn to say "no" gracefully;
resist the temptation to chase after more pleasures,
hobbies, and more social entanglements.
Then hold the line with the tenacity
of a tackle for a professional football team.

DR. JAMES DOBSON

Since we live by the Spirit,
let us keep in step with the Spirit.

GALATIANS 5:25 NIV

Temple Treasure

We have this treasure from God,
but we are like clay jars that hold the treasure.
This shows that the great power is from God, not from us.

2 CORINTHIANS 4:7 NCV

It's hard to buy even a jar of peanut butter without scanning the row of magazines by the register. Without turning a single page, the message of each one is clear: the more beautiful you are, the better life is. It's hard not to get sucked into the tempting taglines below the photos of such glamorous people, each promising to give you the one secret you need to know to be beautiful yourself.

But the Bible has already spilled the beans. God's people are gorgeous. But how can such a varied crew of Christians, with all our differing body sizes, shapes, and fashion styles, all boast of beauty? It's not just in the eye of the Beholder. It's who we be holding! God reminds us that our bodies are just jars of clay—pots, of sorts, that He has fashioned for His purpose. When we invite God into our lives, those old clay pots take on the brilliant beauty of heaven, because God Himself lives inside us. Our hearts can't help but shine out His love and grace everywhere we go. And what's more beautiful than that?

Jesus, thank You for filling me with Your Spirit. You make me beautiful!

My hope is to see this generation produce a group
of Christians who will infiltrate our society—
in fact, our entire world—with a pure,
beautiful message of grace and honesty in the marketplace.

CHARLES R. SWINDOLL

Your beauty should come from within you—
the beauty of a gentle and quiet spirit that will
never be destroyed and is very precious to God.

1 PETER 3:4 NCV

Wearing Grace

God has chosen you and made you his holy people.
He loves you. So you should always clothe yourselves
with mercy, kindness, humility, gentleness, and patience.

COLOSSIANS 3:12 NCV

So what are you going to wear today? The question looms before you every morning as you check your calendar and consider which kind of clothing would be most appropriate. Hopefully you've washed them and the right outfit is ready to wear.

As followers of Christ, we never have to wonder about our clothes because God gives us daily access to heaven's divine wardrobe. With His Spirit's help, we can find everything we need to fit ourselves with holiness, truth, and love—the kind of character God wants His kids to wear, whether we're going out or staying in. Before we knew Jesus, we were slaves to our old bad habits, such as raging tempers, selfish motives, and uncontrolled tongues. But now as new creations with Christ's Spirit inside us, we are free to walk in God's ways instead. Though it may feel fake or foreign at first, in time our hearts will recognize the truth: our new, God-given attitudes match the beauty of our new Christ-bought identity best.

Jesus, give me the wisdom and grace I need to put on love for this day.

Love as distinct from "being in love" is not merely a feeling. It is a deep unity, maintained by the will and deliberately strengthened by habit.

C. S. LEWIS

Friendship requires a steady, constant, and unchangeable character, a person that is uniform in his intimacy.

PLUTARCH

Treasure Hunt

*Work with enthusiasm, as though you were working
for the Lord rather than for people. Remember that
the Lord will reward each one of us for the good we do.*

EPHESIANS 6:7-8 NLT

If someone handed you a treasure map and promised
you'd find a chest of gold if you followed it, would you?
Even if wild adventures aren't your cup of tea, the pleasure
of reward probably is. God wired us to want something in
return for our efforts. So we work for paychecks. We raise
children to see them succeed in life. We exercise to earn
fit bodies. So is it a surprise that God promises to reward
us when we walk in the good works He has planned for us?
It's all part of God's spectacular plan to bless His kids, not
only now as we obey His lead here on earth but in heaven,
too, where every good deed translates into a divine reward.

If you know God is watching and waiting to bless your
acts of obedience, each day becomes an adventure with
God's Word as the treasure map leading you to divine riches. God has hidden moments in each day for you to discover how to encourage and support others and grow the
kingdom. The more we spend of ourselves for God's glory,
the richer we are in Jesus!

Father, show me where to go and what to do to be a blessing
to someone else today.

After the friendship of God, a friend's affection
is the greatest treasure here below.

ANONYMOUS

Among [our] treasures [are] such wonderful
things as the grace of Christ, the love of Christ,
the joy and peace of Christ.

L. B. COWMAN

Summer Storms

*Then they cried out to the LORD in their trouble,
and he brought them out of their distress.
He stilled the storm to a whisper; the waves of the sea
were hushed. They were glad when it grew calm,
and he guided them to their desired haven.*

PSALM 107:28–30 NIV

If you live in the South, you know how fast the weather can change. Billowy cumulus clouds build high in the day's heat and then dump their fat raindrops right onto whatever you've got going on. Southerners just learn to either take an umbrella or simply sit it out for a while, knowing the sun's not far away.

Christians all over the world would do well to learn a similar life application. When Jesus promised to leave His peace with us, He didn't imply living in a pain-free world. In fact, He reminds us that "In this world you will have trouble" (John 16:33 NIV). Christians are not immune to life's storms. God even ordains them to develop our trust in Him.

But we can respond to the rain with hope, anchored by God's faithfulness. God Himself is our shelter, our safe place, during our trials. He keeps us safe. And we can wait patiently for these times to pass, because we know summer storms don't last forever. God has promised us a future and a hope beyond our wildest dreams. If we wait on God to do what He promised, we won't be disappointed.

Lord, when the rains come into my life, I will find my shelter in You and wait for You to save me.

I need Thy presence every passing hour;
What but Thy grace can foil the tempter's power?
Who like Thyself my guide and stay can be?
Through cloud and sunshine, O abide with me.
I fear no foe, with Thee at hand to bless;
Ills have no weight, and tears no bitterness:
Where is death's sting? Where, grave, thy victory?
I triumph still, if Thou abide with me.

HENRY FRANCIS LYTE

The best friendships have weathered
misunderstandings and trying times.
One of the secrets of a good relationships
is the ability to accept the storms.

ALAN LOY MCGINNIS

Follow the Leader

He will feed his flock like a shepherd. He will carry the lambs in his arms, holding them close to his heart.

ISAIAH 40:11 NLT

Children don't have any trouble understanding the game. They love to play "Follow the Leader" because it keeps them moving and going in unexpected places and ways, but they always know what to do since the leader shows them.

When Jesus said that the best approach to God's kingdom is one of childlike faith, He meant it. Following Jesus's lead is not much different than the children's game—only it's for a lifetime and not just a few moments. Jesus identifies Himself as our Shepherd because He's in charge and knows where He wants to take us. He has understanding and wisdom that we, His little lambs, simply do not. But we don't have to worry about all of our weaknesses or try to control the herd around us, either. God's got it all under His control. All we need to do is keep our eyes focused on Jesus and follow in His footsteps. He will nourish us, protect us, and keep us close to His heart everywhere we go.

Lord, thank You for leading me throughout life. You are my Great Shepherd and I will follow You.

My Good Shepherd, who have shown Your very gentle
mercy to us...give grace and strength to me,
Your little lamb, that in no tribulation or anguish
or pain may I turn away from You.

JULIAN OF NORWICH

You can't grow closer without investing
in the relationship. That's how it works with God too.
He didn't make us robots, pre-programmed to love
Him and follow Him. He gave us free will and leaves
it to us to choose to spend time with Him.
That way it's genuine. That way it's a real relationship.

TOM RICHARDS

A blessed thing it is for any
man or woman to have a friend,
one human soul whom we can trust
utterly, who knows the best
and worst of us, and who loves us
in spite of all our faults.

CHARLES KINGSLEY

Reaping Redemption

So let's not get tired of doing what is good. At just the right time we will reap a harvest of blessing if we don't give up.

GALATIANS 6:9 NLT

Movies, particularly dramas, move our hearts. Within approximately two hours of time, we sit captive to an unfolding story of tragedy and heartbreak, resolved through some sort of magnificent redemption in the end, revealing a hidden beauty in the journey. But as we wipe away our tears and turn back to the real world and real life, we realize the pain of the growth process is hard. *Where is the redemption of all our efforts to pray and do good for ourselves and our loved ones?* we can't help but wonder.

Jesus tells us it rests with Him. He urges us to press on in doing the good we do—not to demand our goals be met, but to bring honor to Him as we serve. He is our prize, and relationship with Him builds as we trust Him in the waiting. He has promised that His Word will not return void but will accomplish everything He intends for it. Our prayers prayed according to that Word will be answered with "yes!" one day. Our real-life stories aren't finished yet, the plot is still unwinding in each moment. We will enjoy the gradual reveal more when we rest in the Author's ability to work out all the elements for a grand, redemptive end.

Father, You declare the end from the beginning. I look expectantly to You as I watch You work faithfully in and through my life.

C*harity is never lost: it may meet with ingratitude,
or be of no service to those on whom it was bestowed,
yet it ever does a work of beauty and grace upon the
heart of the giver.*

CONYERS MIDDLETON

F*riendship requires deeds.*

JOHANNES STOBAEUS

S*ee, I am doing a new thing! Now it springs up;
do you not perceive it? I am making a way
in the wilderness and streams in the wasteland.*

ISAIAH 43:19 NIV

Bound to Love

The Lord appeared to us in the past, saying:
"I have loved you with an everlasting love;
I have drawn you with unfailing kindness."

JEREMIAH 31:3 NIV

You knew your world would never be the same after that first encounter. Something about him drew you in, a calling to experience adventure and romance your soul had always yearned to answer. Living for yourself had lost all its luster. Now all you wanted was to lavish your love on the one who held your heart.

And so it is with love. When we truly love someone, we gladly give all of ourselves—knowing our greatest joy lies in that sacred connection.

And so it is in our relationship with Jesus, the essence and eminence of all true love. In love, He offers restoration and reconciliation with God for free. With no strings attached, we are free to receive His eternal love.

But then the catch! Once we have tasted God's goodness, felt the warmth of His embrace, and heard His song sung over our lives, our hearts are never the same. We can never go back, nor would we ever want to. We are bound to love Him back—not out of duty but in purest delight.

Lord, one day in Your courts is better than a thousand elsewhere. You are the love of my soul!

We are told to make love our aim,
and we are given the grace and insight
to do it by the God who created our minds
and who demonstrated love before us all on His cross.

EUGENIA PRICE

Grace binds you with far stronger cords than
the cords of duty or obligation can bind you.
Grace is free, but when once you take it,
you are bound forever to the Giver and bound
to catch the spirit of the Giver. Like produces like.
Grace makes you gracious, the Giver makes you give.

E. STANLEY JONES

Cause and Effect

People harvest only what they plant. If they plant to satisfy
their sinful selves, their sinful selves will bring them ruin.
But if they plant to please the Spirit, they will receive
eternal life from the Spirit.

GALATIANS 6:7-8 NCV

We know our world operates by cause and effect, a concept easily seen in nature around us. If we touch a hot stove, we recoil in pain. If we jump up in the air, we know we'll come down. But often we don't realize that the same kind of principles work in the spiritual realm, as well. What we sow in our soul will grow out in our actions at some point down the road.

So God tells us to guard our hearts and minds. Be careful about what kinds of images, music, and words you allow in. Be intentional to sow thoughts that are true, gracious, and thankful.

How would you describe your attitude lately? Understanding grace always yields a heart filled with gratitude. If you find yourself struggling with discontent and doubt, trace the symptoms back to their unbelieving source, and choose to sow seeds of truth in your mind instead. Remember and revel in God's amazing grace, and watch in wonder as your grateful heart grows.

Father, forgive me when I forget to thank You for Your grace. You are so good to me!

Grace and gratitude belong together
like heaven and earth.
Grace evokes gratitude
like the voice an echo.
Gratitude follows grace
as thunder follows lightning.

KARL BARTH

Nothing taken for granted; everything received
with gratitude; everything passed on with grace.

G. K. CHESTERTON

Empty Spaces

*The Lord All-Powerful is with us;
the God of Jacob is our defender. Selah*

PSALM 46:7 NCV

Sometimes it's as plain as the empty messages and inbox app on your phone. Other times it's an inexplicable inner gnawing on your soul. No matter who you call or where you go, you simply can't shake feeling lonely. Left to fester, loneliness can easily lead to depression or unhealthy coping habits.

But it doesn't have to. Loneliness can also be looked at as an invitation. If we let it, the empty spaces in our souls become the perfect filling spot for God's Spirit. Instead of stuffing ourselves with activities or material goods to stop the pain, God invites us to come to Him for our soul's satisfaction. He longs to soothe our aching hearts with the power and beauty of His presence, His Spirit filling that void. Suddenly we realize that God Himself is with us, everywhere we go. We have a constant companion who listens and cares—and always will, for all of eternity. Loneliness is life's gentle reminder that we all long for real relationship that lasts forever...and we find that friend in Jesus.

Lord, thank You for the lonely times because they give me space and time to draw nearer to You.

You have made us for yourself,
O Lord, and our hearts are restless
until they find their rest in you.

ST. AUGUSTINE

It is a gift to know that you see as another sees,
an immense pleasure to be understood,
to enjoy the easy companionship of one you
can let your guard down with.

JOHN AND STASI ELDREDGE

Life Interruptions

Brothers and sisters, we want you to know
about those Christians who have died so you will not be sad,
as others who have no hope. We believe that Jesus died
and that he rose again. So, because of him,
God will raise with Jesus those who have died.

1 THESSALONIANS 4:13-14 NCV

For years, you had invested time and energy into making new friends. Finally, you found one worth all the effort, one who not only gets you but who likes you back. But today you learned that she is leaving, her husband's job taking them both clear across the country. And you are crushed.

Of course, with social media options these days, we can still keep up connections easier across the miles. But separation always hurts, especially when it's the more permanent kind caused by sickness and death. We know deep in our hearts we were made for so much more than what this life affords us.

And our hearts are right. God put eternity in our souls because we were made for friendship with Him and others that lasts forever. Thankfully, Jesus makes that eternal connection possible. Though we say our good-byes here on this earth, we know we'll resume our relationships with other believers in heaven. Our short time here is just a foretaste of glory to come.

Jesus, thank You for restoring hope and reconciling our relationships now and forever.

Friendships begun in this world can be taken up
again in heaven, never to be broken off.

ST. FRANCES DE SALES

This is not the end, we'll meet again
God's promise will be kept,
But all the same, I feel no shame
in all the tears I've wept.
With God's own grace, I'll see your face
when it is my turn to die.
I loved you so, just that, no more;
for now, I'll say good-bye.

FOREST R. WHATLEY

Wherever we are,
it is our friends that make our world.

HENRY DRUMMOND

Commitment Keepers

He was saying to them all, "If anyone wishes to come after Me, he must deny himself, and take up his cross daily and follow Me."

LUKE 9:23 NASB

Every spring, garden shops fill their aisles with beautiful blooms. And you, certain that this year will be better than your previous performances, pick two potted plants that you plan to keep outside. Will you succeed? It depends on your level of commitment to keep those plants alive! Pruning stems, deadheading flowers, and consistent watering will be required, along with adequate sun.

The same is true for cultivating relationships—another beautiful gift from God that thrives according to the care put into them. If we want our friendships to deepen and develop lasting beauty, we can't neglect them with inattention or apathy.

Jesus Himself warns us to consider the cost of true commitment before we even begin forming a friendship with God. Are we hoping to get by with something artificial that really requires no effort, or do we want a living, beautiful, growing relationship with God and others? If so, are we ready to invest the time and energy needed for roots to grow deep and fragrant petals to unfold?

Today, ask Jesus to help you stay the course and spend the needed time each day to cultivate stronger connections in your life.

Lord, show me how to build strong and lasting relationships, and strengthen me to stay committed.

Love is not a possession but a growth. The heart is a lamp with just oil enough to burn for an hour, and if there be no oil to put in again, its light will go out. God's grace is the oil that fills the lamp of love.

HENRY WARD BEECHER

The heart of a friend is a wondrous thing,
A gift of God most fair;
For the seed of friendship there sprouts and grows
to love and beauty rare....
Bless God for the love of friends so true,
A love akin to His,
Which knows our faults and loves us still;
That's what real friendship is.
The heart of a friend is a wondrous thing,
A gift of God most fair;
May I carefully tend the seed which grows
In friendship's garden there.

PAT LASSEN

Soul Sunrise

*From the rising of the sun to its setting
the name of the LORD is to be praised.*

PSALM 113:3 NASB

You see it first only at earth's edges, the rising light slowly seeping through the black of night. But at the horizon, hope grows along with the colors of dawn as reds and oranges and pinks paint the sky. Soon the sun itself peaks over the hill and into view, its warmth washing over you at once. And with each passing minute, the sun only grows in its brilliance, lighting the sky for the day.

Grace, like the sun, grows in our lives—its enormity and heat always in existence, but experienced in increments as we wake up to its reality in our lives. When we first heard of God's love and forgiveness, we gladly received it and reveled in the new light of truth dawning on our lives. But with each passing day, our relationship with Jesus develops into something deeper, something brighter than we had ever once hoped. The fullness of God's unconditional love and the warmth of His eternal acceptance warms us to our core and changes the course of our day. We no longer walk in the darkness. We live life fully in the blaze of His grace.

God, You are more beautiful than I ever imagined. I praise You and thank You for Your grace!

Grace comes into the soul, as the morning sun
into the world; first a dawning, then a light;
and at last the sun in his full and excellent brightness.

THOMAS ADAMS

Friendships are purer and the more ardent,
the nearer they come to the presence of God,
the Sun not only of righteousness but of love.

WALTER LANDOR

Inner Workings

Do not do wrong to repay a wrong,
and do not insult to repay an insult.
But repay with a blessing, because you yourselves were
called to do this so that you might receive a blessing.

1 PETER 3:9 NCV

You are dumbfounded. The very qualities that drew you to your spouse are now the very irritants that drive you batty. *How can he not see such glaring vices?* you wonder. *How can I get her to change?* you then plot.

But before you draw up your battle plans, pause a moment and rethink your perspective. Which relationships in your life would you rank as perfect? If you're honest, probably none. Each person in our lives—including ourselves—suffers from a sinful nature. Each of us equally depend on God's goodness and grace to live. Even our best friendships fail us at times because we are all fallen people living together in a broken world. Rather than getting bent out of shape over the failures, what if we focused on blessing others instead? What if instead of condemnation, we extended love and grace?

God's grace toward us enables us to love unconditionally. We can be confident that God is at work in all of God's people, producing the change He wants to see. May that change start with us.

Jesus, search my heart and see if there is anything that offends You. Then lead me in Your truth!

The needed change within us is God's work,
not ours. The demand is for an inside job,
and only God can work from the inside.
We cannot attain or earn this righteousness
of the kingdom of God: it is a grace that is given.

RICHARD J. FOSTER

First take the log out of your own eye,
and then you will see clearly to take the speck
out of your brother's eye.

MATTHEW 7:5 NASB

Friendship is a deep oneness
that develops when two people,
speaking the truth in love
to one another, journey together
to the same horizon.

TIM KELLER

Sacred Moments

"May peace be within your walls, and prosperity within your palaces." For the sake of my brothers and my friends, I will now say, "May peace be within you." For the sake of the house of the LORD our God, I will seek your good.

PSALM 122:7-9 NASB

It has taken a month for you to coordinate schedules, but at last the day arrives: dinner with your closest friends—at their house. The moment you step across their threshold you know the night won't disappoint. Immediately you're greeted with the tightest of hugs and ushered into the heart of their home. The smell of something scrumptious lights your senses, and the ambiance of music soothes your ears. Soon you're seated and simultaneously enjoying savory food along with long-awaited conversation. To be honest, it's a slice of heaven served on earth.

Such is the blessing of sweet fellowship with friends, all five senses sampling the goodness of God in the gift. In these sacred moments, we truly stand on holy ground. Friendship and fun, food and festivities all tell the tale of an incredibly gracious God determined to bless our lives with a taste of His goodness. He is here in this moment, lavishing His love on you in every kind of way. Don't miss the miracle! Take off your shoes and enjoy the time, telling God thanks for His indescribable gift.

God, You fill up all of my senses with Your great glory. Thank You for Your constant blessings!

*Listen to your life. See it for the fathomless
mystery that it is. In the boredom and pain
of it no less than in the excitement and gladness:
touch, taste, smell your way to the holy
and hidden heart of it because in the last analysis
all moments are key moments and life itself is grace.*

FREDERICK BUECHNER

When friends meet, hearts warm.

JOHN DAY

The Wonder of Worship

*LORD our Lord, your name is the most wonderful name
in all the earth! It brings you praise in heaven above.*

PSALM 8:1 NCV

You can trace it in the tiny fingers of a newborn child or see it in a shooting star. A flower's perfect symmetry and the roar of a summer storm signal that something more, something supernatural, lies at their core. All of creation tells a story of purposeful design, each piece reflecting the divinity and brilliance of its Creator.

Love and true friendship are equally mysterious and miraculous, their very existence proving a deeper value to life than even creation's magnificent beauty. God has fashioned His works to flourish in the undercurrent of His love pulsating through every part and touching our hearts in the process.

When we marvel at the beauty in nature or recognize greatness in the faces we see each day, we are getting a glimpse of God's divine glory. When we fellowship with His people united by His Spirit, we feel we're not so far from Home. In those moments, let your wonder shift to worship of the One who made it all for His glory and our good!

Jesus, You have created an incredible world filled with evidence of Your wisdom, power, and love.

Dear Lord, grant me the grace of wonder.
Surprise me, amaze me, awe me in every crevice of Your
universe. Delight me to see how Your Christ plays
in ten thousand places to the Father through
the features of men's faces. Each day enrapture me
with Your marvelous things without number.
I do not ask to see the reason for it all;
I ask only to share the wonder of it all.

ABRAHAM JOSHUA HESCHEL

I still find each day too short for all the thoughts
I want to think, all the walks I want to take,
all the books I want to read, and all the friends
I want to see. The longer I live, the more my mind
dwells upon the beauty and the wonder of the world.

JOHN BURROUGHS

Overflow

Good people bring good things out of the good
they stored in their hearts. But evil people bring
evil things out of the evil they stored in their hearts.
People speak the things that are in their hearts.

LUKE 6:45 NCV

When you're thirsty for a soda, chances are you don't head for the sink. Why? Past experience and common sense inform you that sinks pour out water. Their pipes are connected to water lines that pull from large reservoirs of water outside your home. So if you want a soda, you have to get it from the kind of fountain that supplies it.

The same is true in the spiritual realm. If we want to become the kind of people God calls His kids to be, we have to reference the right input. Tapping into our personal reservoirs of determination and self-righteousness only yields a life overflowing with pride. It's like looking for soda to flow out of a water faucet. We come up tasteless every time.

If we want to truly be changed, we must look to God alone as our source of strength. Ask His Spirit to fill us with His presence and renew our minds with truth from God's Word. Fill up on God-focused worship and walk through each day with your eyes turned toward Him. His love can't help but overflow if we stay connected to Him.

Jesus, let my words and actions overflow from a heart that is filled with the joy of Your presence.

If a spring is pure and clear,
then all the streams that flow from it must also be clear.
This is how the soul becomes when it understands
how to live within God's grace.

DAVID HAZARD

I pray that the God who gives hope will fill you with
much joy and peace while you trust in him. Then your
hope will overflow by the power of the Holy Spirit.

ROMANS 15:13 NCV

Progressive Parenting

Because we are his children,
God has sent the Spirit of his Son into our hearts,
prompting us to call out, "Abba, Father."

GALATIANS 4:6 NLT

Yesterday, as you sat in the stands watching your child score the winning goal, your spirit soared. But today, you sit in the principal's office alongside the same child. News isn't good, and you know your child's in trouble. *How can parenting kids bring so much joy and so much pain at the same time?* you wonder. *Is there any way to really do it right?*

Since families are God's idea and He has the wisdom and experience we lack, we would do well to watch what He does as our heavenly Father. Once He has adopted us into His family through faith in Jesus, there's no going back—no casting out of His kids, even if they end up in the proverbial principal's office time and time again. God gives us both grace and truth every time we need direction: grace to cover the messes we make, and truth that tells us who we really are as His children. Only then can we change course and live according to our Father's ways.

Next time you see your own kids struggling with sin, remember God's great grace and thank Him for how He parents you in it. Then point your kids to the same source of hope and forgiveness we only find in Jesus.

Father, Your great mercy and grace move me to repentance. Thank You for making me Your child forever!

Lord, it's an awesome job, this parenting thing.
Give me the grace, goodness, and determination
I need to do the best possible job, no matter how tired
or frustrated I get. It's up to You and me, Lord.
Be with me every step of the way.

PATRICIA LORENZ

See how very much our Father loves us,
for he calls us his children, and that is what we are!

1 JOHN 3:1 NLT

I don't think there is anyone who needs God's help
and grace as much as I do. Sometimes I feel so helpless
and weak. I think that is why God uses me.

J. I. PACKER

Breathing in Grace

Therefore, my beloved, as you have always obeyed,
not as in my presence only, but now much more
in my absence, work out your own salvation
with fear and trembling; for it is God who works
in you both to will and to do for His good pleasure.

PHILIPPIANS 2:11–13 NKJV

You're doing it right now, even as you read these words. Without a conscious thought, your lungs are expanding and contracting, drawing in life-giving oxygen, and then breathing out carbon dioxide you don't need (but plants and trees do)! It's just one of God's incredible, life-giving systems taking place in and through us at all times even though we hardly ever take notice.

Just like the air we breathe, God's work in our lives and world surges through our souls often sight unseen. We can't fathom how the mundane details of our day could possibly work toward eternal glory, but God says they do when we commit our day-to-day to Him. Every act of kindness, every prayer prayed, every humble gift of service is seen by our ever-present heavenly Father. He works through our obedience—breathing in His Spirit and exhaling His love to the world—to restore the beauty and redeem the lost people of this world.

So as you start this day, take a deep breath—and relax. God is already at work to make the most of today's moments as you lean on Him for His grace.

Father, You never stop working on my behalf and for the world You love. Thank You for Your faithfulness in all that You do!

Grace needs to be the air we breathe,
the atmosphere we live in,
whether in church or in the home.

ALLEN SNAPP

There is nothing but God's grace.
We walk upon it; we breathe it;
we live and die by it;
it makes the nails and axles of the universe.

ROBERT LOUIS STEVENSON

Daily Bread

Give us each day our daily bread.

LUKE 11:3 NIV

God gave the Israelites clear instructions when He rained down manna from heaven each day into the dry wilderness below. They were to go out, gather just enough for themselves and their families, and use up what they'd been given. No saving or hoarding was allowed, except for the day before Sabbath when they could gather twice as much to tide them over for the day of rest. It was a simple command to develop childlike dependence on God who gave them what they needed for each day.

Thousands of years later, Jesus explained the deeper significance of daily seeking God's sustenance. The lesson was not just for the Israelites back then but for all of God's children as we wander through the wilderness of life. Jesus revealed that He Himself is our manna, our bread from heaven, come down to give us all that we need of His power, His grace, His forgiveness every day.

Just as our bodies need physical food each day for energy, our souls need the nourishment that only comes from seeking Jesus daily and ingesting His goodness into our lives.

Jesus, thank You for being the answer to all my needs and for providing life-giving power to me each day.

A man can no more take in a supply of grace
for the future than he can eat enough today to last him
for the next six months, nor can he inhale sufficient air
into his lungs with one breath to sustain life for a week
to come. We are permitted to draw upon God's store
of grace from day to day as we need it.

DWIGHT L. MOODY

If God wants you to do something,
He'll make it possible for you to do it,
but the grace He provides comes only
with the task and cannot be stockpiled beforehand.
We are dependent on Him from hour to hour,
and the greater our awareness of this fact,
the less likely we are to faint or fail in a crisis.

LOUIS CASSELS

I*f you go looking for a friend,*
you're going to find they're very scarce.
If you go out to be a friend,
you'll find them everywhere.

ZIG ZIGLAR

Unoffendable

A person's wisdom yields patience;
it is to one's glory to overlook an offense.

PROVERBS 19:11 NIV

You didn't mean to say it. You were at your wit's end, stressed out and stretched thin, and before you knew it you had spoken some of the most careless, hurtful words to the friend who was trying to help you the most. Shame and fear filled you simultaneously as you wondered what the repercussions of your impulsivity would be. But your friend blew you away—not in retaliation or an angry tirade, but in unmitigated grace and forgiveness...then simply resumed being your friend.

Forgiveness is the defining hallmark of the truest, richest friendships. Loyalty that always looks for the best in others and overlooks their faults as much as possible follows close behind. If we want to be like Jesus, we must adopt His grace-filled perspective, the perspective that saw past our faults to the promise of perfected fellowship with His people. May we each be like Jesus, unoffendable in our relationships with others, seeking to pull out the best in everyone we encounter.

Jesus, I am amazed by Your relentless grace and mercy toward me, an unworthy sinner. Help me to show that same forgiveness and love toward others.

Among the most powerful of human experiences
is to give or to receive forgiveness....
Forgiveness is a collapsing into the mystery of God
as totally unearned love, unmerited grace.
It is the final surrender to the humility and power
of a Divine Love and a Divine Lover.

RICHARD ROHR

Good friends are good forgivers.

ANONYMOUS

Great Expectations

These two things cannot change: God cannot lie when
he makes a promise, and he cannot lie when he makes an oath.
These things encourage us who came to God for safety.
They give us strength to hold on to the hope we have been given.
We have this hope as an anchor for the soul, sure and strong.

HEBREWS 6:18–19 NCV

You can feel it in the air, even clearer than the crisp winter winds now swirling around. Of course, it's hard to miss the endless carols playing on the radio and the colorful lights bedazzling homes and stores alike, heralding the Christmas season. But the feeling of anticipation is palpable, the advent of something new, something right, something that just feels like home is right around the corner.

For Christians, that day is coming. The same Savior whose birth we celebrate on Christmas is planning the most spectacular homecoming this universe has ever seen. No matter what difficulties beset us here, God's people always hold the hope of glory that awaits us in heaven—the promise of new, eternal, perfect bodies and souls, with spirits united forever to the God who made us, loves us, and lives within us forever! With such an incredible inheritance awaiting us, we can live each day with excited anticipation—like kids at Christmas. Let the countdown begin!

Jesus, I long for the day when all will be made right and we will enjoy perfect friendships with You and Your people forever!

All are friends in heaven, all faithful friends,
And many friendships in the days of Time
Begun, are lasting there and growing still.

SIR FREDERICK POLLOCK

Grace means God sending His only Son to the cross
to descend into hell so that we guilty ones might be
reconciled to God and received into heaven.

J. I. PACKER

Firm Foundation

That person is like a man building a house who dug deep and laid the foundation on rock. When the floods came, the water tried to wash the house away, but it could not shake it, because the house was built well.

LUKE 6:48 NCV

Standing on the shore of the California coastline, you feel the stinging cold as waves wash over your feet. Though you stand tall and still, the rhythmic tide tears at the sand, shifting your stance and your balance. If you plan to stand for long, it's best to seek better footing on the massive rocks imbedded nearby. Waves may crash there, but the foundation remains unmoved.

And so it is with Jesus. In a world of constant change and shifting morals, we have a place where we can stand unmoved by the pressures of the world. Jesus doesn't just know the truth. Scripture tells us that He IS the truth. When we seek a personal relationship with Him by submitting to His teaching and inviting His Spirit to live inside us, our souls find a permanent foundation that cannot be shaken.

As you consider your life, do you feel the power of today's culture causing your beliefs and values to shift? If so, step out of the sand and onto the Rock of Ages, the God whose truth never changes. Discover what it feels like to stand tall and secure through the ebbs and flows of life.

God, You are absolute truth. I find my bearings when I stand on Your Word and follow Your ways.

Our Savior pictures Himself not merely as the Rock of Ages, and our Strong Rock of Refuge, but the Rock of our Salvation. Here, in Him and upon His merit and atoning grace, we were saved from among the lost.

CHARLES HURLBURT AND T. C. HORTON

How Sweet the name of Jesus...
the rock on which I build,
my shield and hiding place,
my never failing treasury,
filled with boundless stores of grace.

JOHN NEWTON

Known

The time is coming—indeed it's here now—
when true worshipers will worship the Father
in spirit and in truth. The Father is looking
for those who will worship him that way.

JOHN 4:23 NLT

Webster says the word "known" is an adjective, defined as "to have established or fixed in the mind or memory." In the context of our good friends, though, to be known means so much more. It implies a knowledge that goes far deeper than political opinions or decorating preferences—though such trivia comprises true knowing. But our very best friends see more into our soul, knowing the heart behind our actions and loving us for the people we are.

And that is what makes Jesus our very best Friend. Unlike any other person on earth, Jesus knows us because He made us! Before a word is even on our tongues, God knows what we'll say. He understands our past and holds our future. We will never be known by anyone as fully as our God knows and loves us.

But friendship is a two-way street. God, too, wants us to know who He really is. He's not satisfied by a casual acquaintance. He seeks worshippers who want to know and love Him back, in Spirit and in truth. And He isn't hard to find. God opens His heart to us through His Word and gives us understanding through His Spirit. Ask Him for grace today to know your Best Friend better.

Jesus, I want to know You more. Please open the eyes of my heart and mind to understand and believe Your love and truth.

God is not some remote, unknowable deity, a prisoner in His aloofness or shut up in His solitariness, but on the contrary the God who is free to go outside of Himself, to share in the life of His creatures and enable them to share in His own eternal Life.

THOMAS TORRANCE

O Lord, you have examined my heart
and know everything about me.
You know when I sit down or stand up.
You know my thoughts even when I'm far away.
You see me when I travel
and when I rest at home.
You know everything I do.
You know what I am going to say
even before I say it, Lord.
You go before me and follow me.
You place your hand of blessing on my head.
Such knowledge is too wonderful for me,
too great for me to understand!

PSALM 139:1-6 NLT

Parasite Problems

*Let us throw off everything that hinders
and the sin that so easily entangles. And let us run
with perseverance the race marked out for us.*

HEBREWS 12:1 NIV

Your dog has cuddled up to you, loving your petting and licking you in response, when suddenly you feel something foreign. Upon further investigation, you're suddenly grossed out. *How and when did that tick get there?* you wonder as you question whether you gave your pup his prevention medicine this month. Regardless, you know the tick has got to go if you want to keep your dog healthy.

The same is true for idols in our lives. An idol is anything we allow into our lives that sucks the life out of us—the life of holiness and devotion to God we were created to live. When we make certain friends or relationships or careers or achievements more important to us than our relationship with God, we have a spiritual parasite that can wreak all kinds of havoc. We can't let them stay if we want to be healthy spiritually.

So what is the cure? Replace the life-sucking problem with a life-giving solution. Our souls were designed for God alone to satisfy our deepest needs for purpose, love, and affirmation.

Lord, I want to love You alone with all my heart, soul, mind, and strength. Please keep me from putting anything or anyone before You.

Grace is not simply leniency when we have sinned.
Grace is the enabling gift of God not to sin.
Grace is power, not just pardon.

JOHN PIPER

I am the Lord; that is my name!
I will not give my glory to anyone else,
nor share my praise with carved idols.

ISAIAH 42:8 NLT

Hold On

Hold on to what is good.

1 THESSALONIANS 5:21 NLT

Darkness didn't just fall across the land when Jesus died that day on the cross. The hope and joy of all His followers fell with it, their light snuffed out by Satan's cruel scheme. So what were the women who followed Jesus doing at dawn of that third day? The only thing they knew to do: honoring Jesus's body by dressing Him with spices.

But that's when more than just the sun arose, casting light to dispel the darkness. Jesus defied death, conquered hell, and resurrected to His rightful place as King of kings. Mary, who encountered the risen Jesus first, simply clung to His feet in worship. She—like all the other followers who later saw Him, too—didn't understand everything that was happening, but she knew one thing for certain: Jesus is God, her Savior and Friend.

No matter how dark our days may seem or how hopeless our situations appear, we hold this same hope. Our Savior is real, He is near, and He is our forever Friend. The darkness has been pierced by an eternal light. So hold onto Jesus until we see clearly, on that day when all will be restored and every relationship made right.

Jesus, I can't thank You enough for saving me and choosing me to be Your friend. I'm holding onto You, even as I know that You are holding me.

Lord, I praise You. I magnify Your name.
I am daily amazed by Your grace and mercy.
You are the heart of my life. Without You my life
is incomplete. With You I have everything I need.
I worship and praise Your name. Amen.

MARILYN JANSEN

Do you see His wondrous face?
Full of glory, love and grace?
Look, and all thy need confess,
Worship His pure Holiness.

CHARLES HURLBURT AND T. C. HORTON

He is altogether lovely. This is my beloved,
and this is my friend.

SONG OF SOLOMON 5:16 KJV

The dearest friend

on earth is a mere shadow

compared to Jesus Christ.

OSWALD CHAMBERS